WHO WOULD WIN?®

FALCON

VS.

HAWK

BY
JERRY PALLOTTA

ILLUSTRATED BY
ROB BOLSTER

Scholastic Inc.

*The publisher would like to thank the following for their
kind permission to use their photographs in this book:*

Photos ©: **Shutterstock:** *4 amur (aDam Wildlife), 4 peregrine (outdoorsman),
4 gyrfalcon (Bildagentur Zoonar GmbH), 4 barbary (Agami Photo Agency),
5 red-tailed (Chris Hill), 5 goshawk (Jesus Giraldo Gutierrez),
5 harris (Timothy M Olsen), 5 cooper's (Ian Maton), 5 osprey (Lone Wolf Photography),
7 (Don Mammoser), 8 top (Ondrej Prosicky), 8 bottom (Ken Griffiths),
9 top (Ian Duffield), 32 (Agnieszka Bacal),* **United States Mint:** *19 coin.*

To my favorite falcon, Rose Wandelmaier.
—J.P.
To the favorite falcon's loving family.
—R.B.

Text copyright © 2020 by Jerry Pallotta.
Illustrations copyright © 2020 by Rob Bolster.

ISBN: 978-1-338-32026-8

11 10   22 23 24

Printed in the U.S.A.   40
First printing, 2020

What would happen if a falcon met up with a hawk? What if they had a fight? Who do you think would win?

HELLO, FALCONS

Falcons, hawks, owls, kites, and eagles are raptors. Raptors are animals that kill other animals and eat them.

There are several species of falcons:

Amur Falcon

Peregrine Falcon

WING FACT
Birds have two wings.

Gyrfalcon

Barbary Falcon

Black Falcon

FACT
All birds have feathers.

Grey Falcon

Prairie Falcon

Falcons are also called birds of prey. They catch their dinner. They eat meat.

HELLO, HAWKS

Hawks are also raptors and birds of prey. Some birds eat seeds, and some birds eat fruit. Hawks eat meat. Here are several kinds of hawks:

Red-tailed Hawk

Goshawk

Harris's Hawk

Common Black Hawk

Cooper's Hawk

NAME FACT
Buzzards, harriers, and kites are also hawks.

FACT
An Osprey is also called a Seahawk.

Zone-tailed Hawk

Osprey

MEET THE FALCON

Here is the Peregrine Falcon.
Scientific name: *Falco peregrinus*

fastest animal
on Earth

This bird is built for speed. It can dive at more than 200 miles per hour. It is the fastest animal on Earth when diving.

A cheetah can run up to 70 miles per hour.

fastest
fish

fastest
land
animal

A sailfish can swim up to 90 miles per hour.

The fastest Olympic sprinters run up to 27 miles per hour.

fastest
humans

MEET THE HAWK

Here is a Red-tailed Hawk.
Scientific name: *Buteo jamaicensis*

To see a Red-tailed Hawk, look in high, bare branches along a road. Red-tailed Hawks want to be able to see in all directions. They are constantly looking to avoid predators and to catch prey.

When hawks see an animal on the ground, they swoop down and try to catch it with their talons.

> **DEFINITION**
> *A talon is a long, sharp, curved claw. People do not have talons.*

AIR

Falcons look for birds to capture and eat. The Peregrine Falcon attacks in the air at high speeds beak first, then catches prey with its claws. The Peregrine eats various prey, including smaller, slower, and weaker birds.

GROUP FACT
A group of birds is called a flock.

FACT
The home of a bird is called a nest. Falcons build a simple nest called a scrape.

A falcon often builds its nest in a crevice high on a cliff.

GROUND

Hawks attack from the air to the ground feet first. They grab and stab prey with their long, sharp talons.

HOME FACT
A Red-tailed Hawk usually builds its nest high in the crown of a tree.

Hawks look for mice, rats, voles, moles, frogs, lizards, and other small animals to eat.

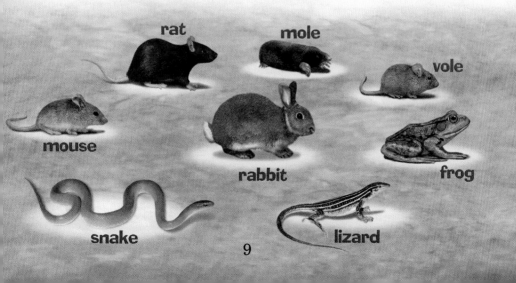

rat

mole

vole

mouse

rabbit

frog

snake

lizard

LARGEST

The largest living bird is the Common Ostrich. It stands up to 9 feet tall but is flightless.

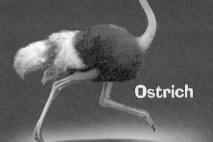

FOOD FACT
People eat ostrich. The meat looks and tastes like beef.

Ostrich

The largest extinct bird is the Elephant Bird. Scientists believe it stood up to 10 feet tall and weighed up to 1,000 pounds. The tallest extinct bird is the Moa. It stood up to 12 feet tall.

DEFINITION
Extinct means that a species is no longer alive.

Elephant Bird

Moa

The largest flying seabird is the Wandering Albatross. Its 12-foot wingspan is longer than any living flying bird.

SMALLEST

The smallest living bird is the Bee Hummingbird. It is the size of a large bee.

Bee Hummingbird

Common Ostrich egg ↘

EGG FACT

The smallest bird has the smallest bird egg. It is smaller than a single coffee bean.

Chicken egg ↙

actual sizes

Bee Hummingbird egg ↙

11

HOW

The shape of an airplane wing and the shape of a bird's wing are similar. Air flows over the top of the wing faster than air flows across the bottom. This creates lift. Lift allows planes and birds to take flight.

LIFT

low pressure

wing side-view

airflow

high pressure

SEA FACT
Penguins are birds that do not fly in the sky. But if you watch them swim in the ocean, they seem to fly underwater.

FACT
Wilbur and Orville Wright studied birds and bird-wing structure before designing the first airplane.

12

WINGS WORK

Another way to create lift is to adjust the front of the wing upward. This causes drag on the back end.

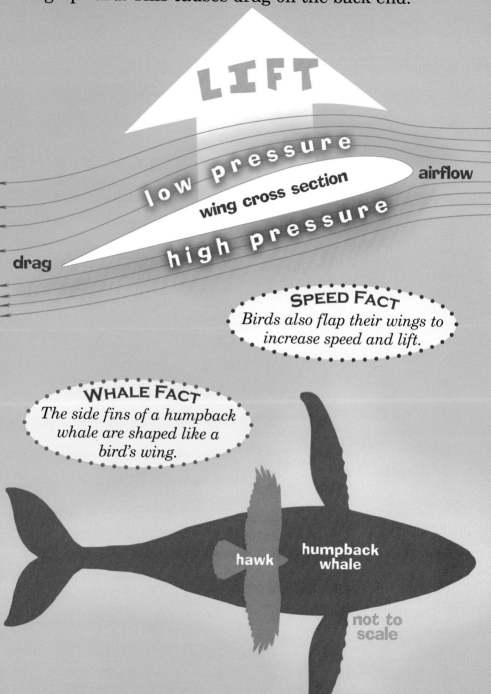

LIFT

low pressure

airflow

wing cross section

high pressure

drag

SPEED FACT
Birds also flap their wings to increase speed and lift.

WHALE FACT
The side fins of a humpback whale are shaped like a bird's wing.

hawk

humpback whale

not to scale

Falcons have excellent eyesight. Like most birds of prey, they have better vision than a human being.

DID YOU KNOW?
A falcon cannot move its eyes.

Falcons can see tiny animals from about one mile away. In the sky, a falcon can see other birds before they see it.

Hawks also have great eyesight. Hawks see little animals on the ground that humans could never see without binoculars.

IDIOM
"Eyes like a hawk" is an expression for having excellent vision.

DID YOU KNOW?
A hawk also can't move its eyes the way we do. A hawk moves its entire head to follow what it wants to see.

BEAK

A Peregrine Falcon's greatest weapons are its speed and beak. Its beak is pointed and sharp but also has a tooth-shaped edge.

SHARP FACT
A falcon's hooked beak is used to rip flesh.

DID YOU KNOW?
You can identify what a bird eats by the shape of its beak.

BONUS FACT
Some birds have special beaks for cracking seeds, sipping nectar, and catching insects.

BILL

The Red-tailed Hawk has a sharp beak that is designed to tear and rip skin and meat.

DEFINITION
A bill is another word for beak.

FACT
All birds have beaks.

DESIGN FACT
Other birds have beaks for chiseling trees, catching fish, and straining water.

TALONS

A Peregrine Falcon's talon can be almost an inch long.

TOE FACT
Most birds have four toes on each foot—three in front, one in back.

FOOT

FOUR TOES

TALON

DINO FACT
A T. rex also had three toes in front and one toe in back.

ACTUAL SIZE

UNITED STATES OF AMERICA
IN GOD WE TRUST
LIBERTY
QUARTER DOLLAR

US QUARTER

PEREGRINE FALCON TALON

FEET TUCKED DURING FLIGHT

FEET

A Red-tailed Hawk's talon can measure up to 1.3 inches long.

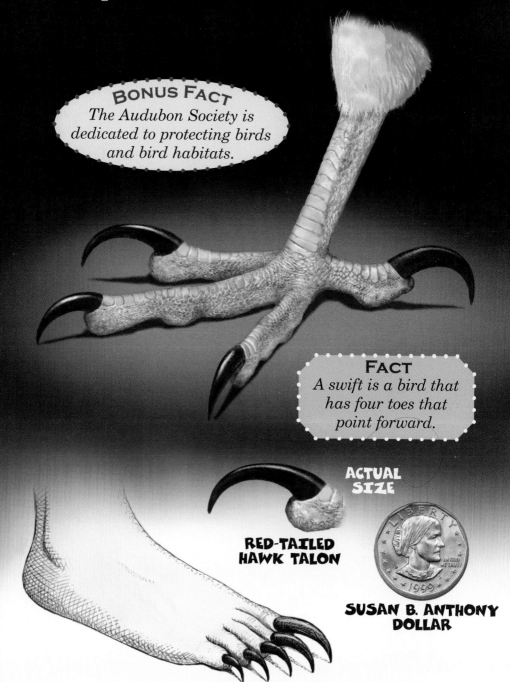

BONUS FACT
The Audubon Society is dedicated to protecting birds and bird habitats.

FACT
A swift is a bird that has four toes that point forward.

ACTUAL SIZE

RED-TAILED HAWK TALON

SUSAN B. ANTHONY DOLLAR

Would you like to have talons instead of toenails?

SPEED

A Peregrine Falcon flies up to 60 miles per hour but it can dive at more than 200 miles per hour. The Peregrine can dive from up to .62 miles in the air.

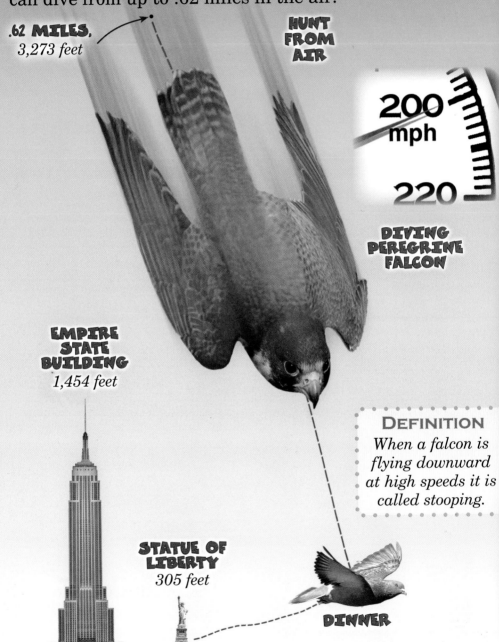

.62 MILES, *3,273 feet*

HUNT FROM AIR

200 mph
220

DIVING PEREGRINE FALCON

EMPIRE STATE BUILDING *1,454 feet*

DEFINITION
When a falcon is flying downward at high speeds it is called stooping.

STATUE OF LIBERTY *305 feet*

DINNER

QUICKNESS

A Red-tailed Hawk flies at about 20-40 miles per hour but can reach a speed of up to 120 miles per hour when diving for food.

HUNT FROM AIR

120 mph   14 mp

DIVING RED-TAILED HAWK

SPORT FACT
Falconry is the sport of training hawks and falcons to hunt in cooperation with a person.

DINNER

HUNT FROM TREE

Red-tailed hawks can spot a mouse from up to 100 feet.

TAIL

An arrow, an airplane, and a jet can't fly without a tail. A falcon also needs its tail to fly. The tail holds steady, or stabilizes, its flight.

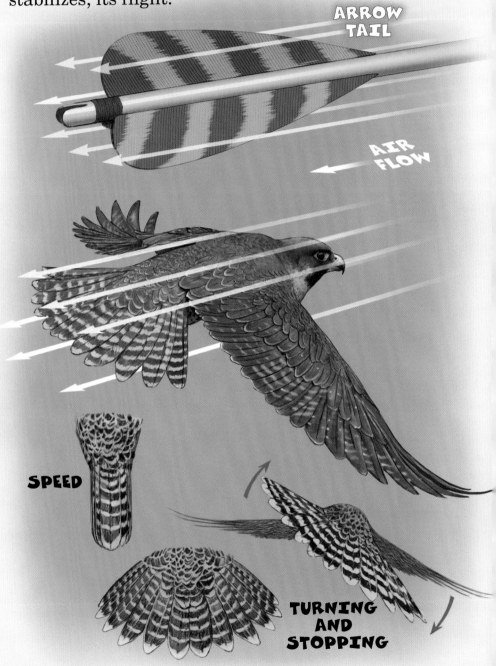

ARROW TAIL

AIR FLOW

SPEED

TURNING AND STOPPING

The falcon also can move its tail to turn or twirl.

TAIL

A Red-tailed Hawk also has a tail. Its tail movement helps the hawk turn left, turn right, dive, or rise.

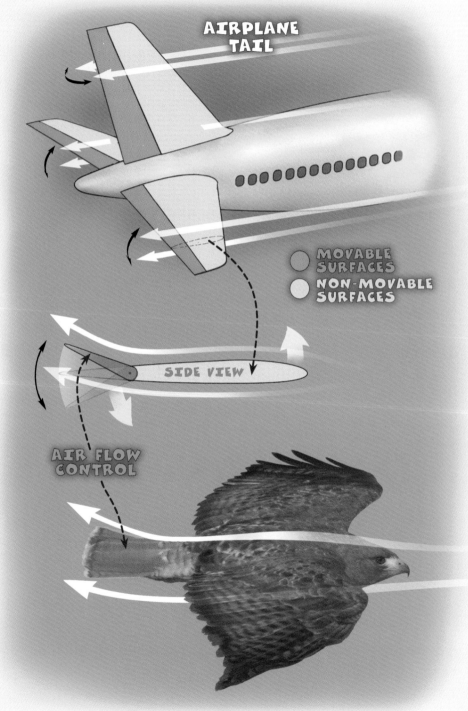

AIRPLANE TAIL

MOVABLE SURFACES

NON-MOVABLE SURFACES

SIDE VIEW

AIR FLOW CONTROL

FALCON WINGS

A falcon's wings are thin and slender. They are built for maximum speed.

DEFINITION
An ornithologist is a scientist who studies birds.

FALCON WEIGHT

FEMALE   **MALE**

An adult female Peregrine Falcon weighs about 3.3 pounds. A male weighs about 2.2 pounds.

HAWK WINGS

The Red-tailed Hawk has wide wings. Its broad wings help it maneuver through trees to grab mice, squirrels, frogs, and other small animals. Hawks have shorter, wider wings than falcons.

BONUS NAME FACT
*Red-tailed Hawks
are sometimes called
roadside hawks.*

HAWK WEIGHT

FEMALE   **MALE**

An adult female Red-tailed Hawk weighs up to 3.2 pounds. A male weighs up to 2.8 pounds. As with falcons, the female is bigger than the male.

FAMOUS FALCONS

We shouldn't be surprised that the US military named one of its best fighter jets after the falcon. It attacks from the air like the bird. It also can quickly change its speed and direction.

F-16 FIGHTING FALCON

There are sports teams named after falcons. The NFL has a team called the Atlanta Falcons.

ATLANTA FALCONS HELMET

FALCON POSTAGE STAMP

FAMOUS HAWKS

There are also sports teams named after hawks. The NFL has a team called the Seattle Seahawks. The NBA has a team called the Atlanta Hawks.

SEATTLE SEAHAWKS LOGO

SEATTLE **SEAHAWKS**

ATLANTA HAWKS LOGO

RED-TAILED HAWK POSTAGE STAMP

NEVIS

Red-tailed Hawk   40¢

The US military has a helicopter called a Black Hawk. It is named after a Native American chief, Black Hawk.

BLACK HAWK HELICOPTER

The Red-tailed Hawk is sitting at the top of a dead tree, looking for mice. Its position is called a perch. The bigger hawk does not see the smaller falcon one thousand feet above her. The Red-tailed Hawk starts to fly.

It is concentrating on looking for food. Maybe there is a tasty baby squirrel down there somewhere. The Red-taile Hawk never looks up.

The Peregrine Falcon sets its eyes on the hawk. It has laser focus. It gets in its stoop position.

The falcon is flying like a rocket.

The hawk doesn't know what hit it! *Wham!* The falcon slices the hawk and breaks one of its wing bones.

As the hawk tries to correct its flight, the falcon makes another dive. It's a direct hit! *Wham* again! The Red-tailed Hawk is falling uncontrollably. It won't recover.

It crashes to the ground, badly wounded.

After a brief fight on the ground, the falcon eats the hawk and brings some of the meat back to its hungry chicks waiting in the nest.

FALCON WINS!

WHO HAS THE ADVANTAGE? CHECKLIST

FALCON		HAWK
☐	Speed	☐
☐	Eyesight	☐
☐	Wing design	☐
☐	Talons	☐
☐	Weight	☐
☐	Beak	☐
☐	Altitude	☐
☐	Attitude	☐

If you were the author, how would you write the ending?